_____

TO

_____

FROM

_____

DATE

PRIORITIES

THE PRIORITY
OF
RELATIONSHIPS

Things are
temporary,
relationships last
forever. Nothing can
replace the time we
spend investing in
the life of another.

ROY LESSIN

As you develop priorities for your life, start with your heart, not your head...with God, not yourself...and with eternity, not time.

Love the Lord your God
with all your heart and
with all your soul and
with all your strength. These
commandments that I give
you today are to be upon
your hearts. Impress them on
your children. Talk about
them when you sit at home
and when you walk
along the road.

DEUTERONOMY 6:5-7

Each memory that includes
time spent with Dad becomes
a treasured part of a
child's heritage.

Fathers, let your heart
follow God, because there's
a little heart that wants
to follow yours!

ROY LESSIN

Fatherhood is at the core
of the universe.

GEORGE MACDONALD

When a man becomes a father
he is given the greatest opportunity
to express the heart of God.

ROY LESSIN

He *will turn the hearts of the fathers to their children, and the hearts of the children to their fathers.*

MALACHI 4:6

The imprint of the father
remains forever on the
heart of the child.

As a father, may your
will be committed to train
your children and may
your example be clear
to guide them.

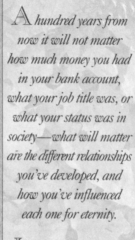

A hundred years from now it will not matter how much money you had in your bank account, what your job title was, or what your status was in society—what will matter are the different relationships you've developed, and how you've influenced each one for eternity.

It is not enough to love those who are near and dear to us. We must show them that we do so.

LORD AVEBURY

Nothing *I have ever done has given me more joys and rewards than being a father to my children.*

BILL COSBY

Happiness is being at peace, being with loved ones, being comfortable. But most of all, it's having those loved ones.

JOHNNY CASH

God has given each of you some
special abilities; be sure to use them to
help each other, passing on to others
God's many kinds of blessings.

1 PETER 4:10 TLB

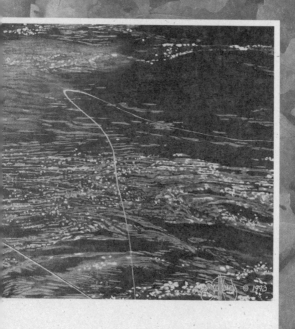

$\mathbb{T}$here is a loftier ambition than
merely to stand high in the world.
It is to stoop down and lift
mankind a little higher.

HENRY VAN DYKE

The goal of much that is written about in life management is to enable us to do more in less time. But is this necessarily a desirable goal? Perhaps we need to get less done, but the right things.

JEAN FLEMING

*Slow down awhile!
Push aside the press of the
immediate. Take time today,
if only for a moment, to
lovingly encourage each one
in your family.*

GARY SMALLEY & JOHN TRENT

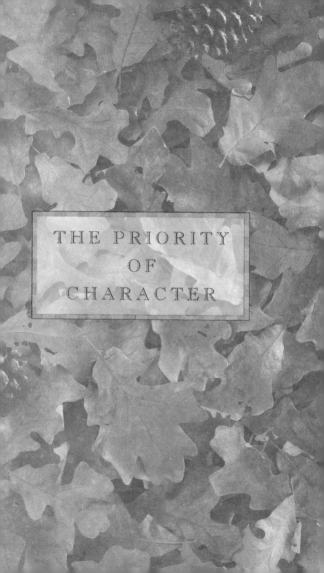

THE PRIORITY
OF
CHARACTER

Character begins on the inside. It's the things we truly value that determine the kind of person we really are.

Things worth remembering:
The value of time,
the success of perseverance,
the pleasure of working,
the dignity of simplicity,
the worth of character,
the improvement of talent,
the influence of example,
the obligation of duty,
the virtue of patience,
the power of kindness.

Finally, brothers, whatever is true, whatever is noble, whatever is right, whatever is pure, whatever is lovely, whatever is admirable— if anything is excellent or praiseworthy—think about such things.

PHILIPPIANS 4:8

A man is what he thinks
about all day long.

RALPH WALDO EMERSON

Our grandest duty
undoubtedly is: not to seek
for that which lies dimly in
the future, but to do that which
lies clearly at hand.

THOMAS CARLYLE

A good man is not a perfect man; a good man is an honest man, faithful and unhesitatingly responsive to the voice of God in his life. The more often he responds to that voice, the easier it is to hear it the next time.

JOHN FISCHER

The important thing is this:
To be ready at any moment
to sacrifice what we are for
what we could become.

CHARLES DUBOIS

He has showed
you, O man, what
is good. And what
does the Lord
require of you?
To act justly and to
love mercy and to
walk humbly with
your God.

MICAH 6:8

I used to think that God's gifts were on shelves one above the other, and that the taller we grew in character the easier we could reach them. I now find that God's gifts are on shelves one beneath the other. It is not a question of growing taller, but of stooping down, to get His best gifts.

F. B. MEYER

Doing is usually connected with a vocation or a career, how we make a living. Being is much deeper. It relates to character, who we are, and how we make a life.

CHARLES R. SWINDOLL

It is the soul that makes a man rich. He is rich or poor according to what he is and not according to what he has.

HENRY WARD BEECHER

Don't lose your grip on Love and Loyalty.... Earn a reputation for living well in God's eyes and the eyes of the people.

PROVERBS 3:1 MSG

You will find as you look back upon your life, that the moments when you have really lived are the moments when you have done things in the spirit of love.

HENRY DRUMMOND

THE PRIORITY
OF
KNOWING GOD

The first priority of every man should be having God at the center of all he is and all he does. If in his heart a man seeks to please God, then every other issue of life will find its proper place. There is nothing that can bring greater joy or fulfillment than to know that you have His smile upon you.

To *have the right priorities*
takes wisdom...
To *live the right priorities*
takes character...
To *keep the right priorities*
takes vision...
To *want the right priorities*
takes love.

ROY LESSIN

We are never more fulfilled than when our longing for God is met by His presence in our lives.

BILLY GRAHAM

It is God's love for us that
He not only gives us His Word
but also lends us His ear. So
it is His work that we do for
our brother when we learn
to listen to Him.

DEITRICH BONHOEFFER

*S*tore up for yourselves treasures in heaven, where moth and rust do not destroy, and where thieves do not break in and steal. For where your treasure is, there your heart will be also.

MATTHEW 6:21

He *is no fool who gives up*
what he cannot keep to gain
what he cannot lose.

JIM ELLIOT

The very possibility
of friendship with
God transforms life,
inevitably deepening
every human
relationship and
making it all vastly
more significant.

Let us examine our capacities and gifts, and then put them to the best use we may. I do not find that we can do better than to put them absolutely in God's hands, and look to Him for the direction of our lives. God can do great things with our lives, if we but give them to Him in sincerity.

ANNA R. B. LINDSAY

"I paint because I feel that's what God wants me to do with the talent He's given me. It's not only a pleasure, but also an act of reverence to paint what I see around me," says Scott Kennedy. A Colorado native and well-known wilderness artist, Kennedy sets the scene for the painting used on this product.

"The Touch"

I like to fish and so do my boys. This is a self-portrait in a way, because it depicts me and my son Ryan. The title refers to the fact that the father is teaching the son that special touch he needs for fly-fishing, but the deeper meaning is the importance of a father's touch in a son's life.

The simplicity of this painting, in terms of color and composition, is very strong. I have invested a lot of emotion in it as well. The original title of the painting was "Learning to Fly." Ryan has just turned eleven, and there's a definite sense that he's launching out on his own. So there's a double meaning in that title too. He's learning to fly both figuratively and literally.

I wanted to do a piece that was simple, graceful, and even elegant. I tried to capture that beauty and the feeling of that moment, early in the morning, with the sun at just the right angle. It's reflecting on the water, the environment, and the two figures, who are sharing a meaningful moment. That is the story I wanted to tell.